Learn the ABCs
Hh
Warren Rylands and Samantha Nugent
LIGHTBOX
openlightbox.com

Go to
www.openlightbox.com
and enter this book's unique code.

ACCESS CODE

LBXQ5642

Lightbox is an all-inclusive digital solution for the teaching and learning of curriculum topics in an original, groundbreaking way. Lightbox is based on National Curriculum Standards.

OPTIMIZED FOR

- ✓ **TABLETS**
- ✓ **WHITEBOARDS**
- ✓ **COMPUTERS**
- ✓ **AND MUCH MORE!**

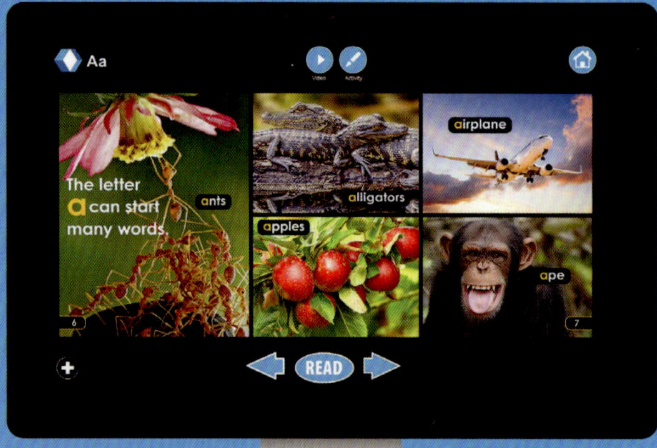

STANDARD FEATURES OF LIGHTBOX

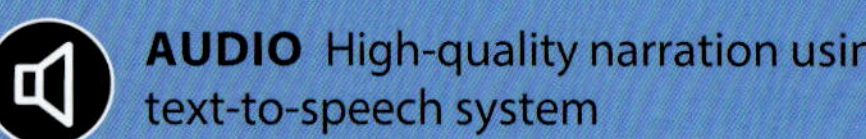
AUDIO High-quality narration using text-to-speech system

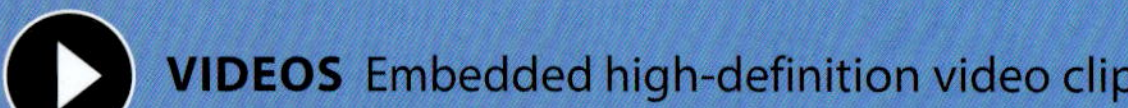
VIDEOS Embedded high-definition video clips

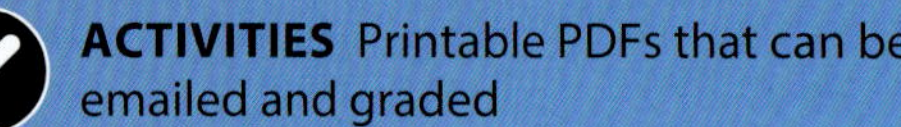
ACTIVITIES Printable PDFs that can be emailed and graded

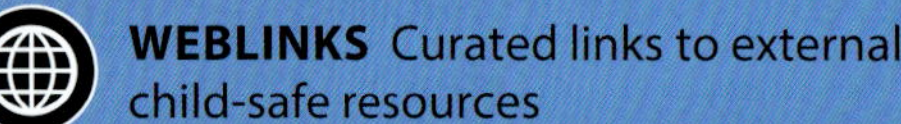
WEBLINKS Curated links to external, child-safe resources

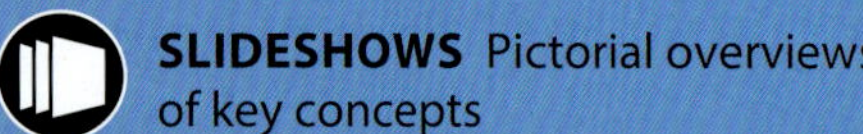
SLIDESHOWS Pictorial overviews of key concepts

INTERACTIVE MAPS Interactive maps and aerial satellite imagery

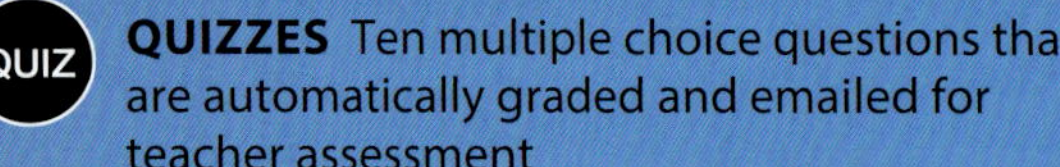
QUIZZES Ten multiple choice questions that are automatically graded and emailed for teacher assessment

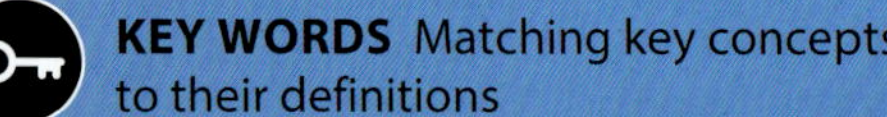
KEY WORDS Matching key concepts to their definitions

VIDEOS

WEBLINKS

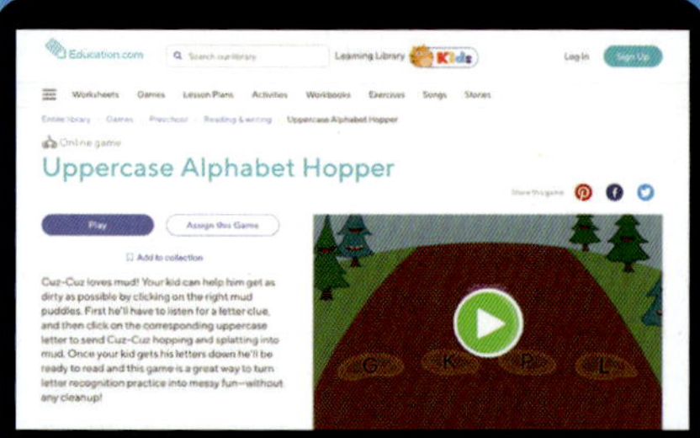

SLIDESHOWS

QUIZZES

This title is part of our Lightbox digital subscription

1-Year K–5 Subscription
ISBN 978-1-5105-5712-3

Access hundreds of Lightbox titles with our digital subscription.
Sign up for a **FREE** subscription trial at **www.openlightbox.com/trial**

Hh

CONTENTS

2 Lightbox Access Code
4 Discovering the Letter H
6 Starting Words with H
8 H Inside a Word
10 Ending Words with H
12 Learning H Names
14 Different H Sounds
16 The H Sound
18 When H Stays Quiet
20 Having Fun with H
22 H and the Alphabet
24 Key Words

Let's discover the letter

This is an uppercase 

This is how you write it

This is a lowercase h

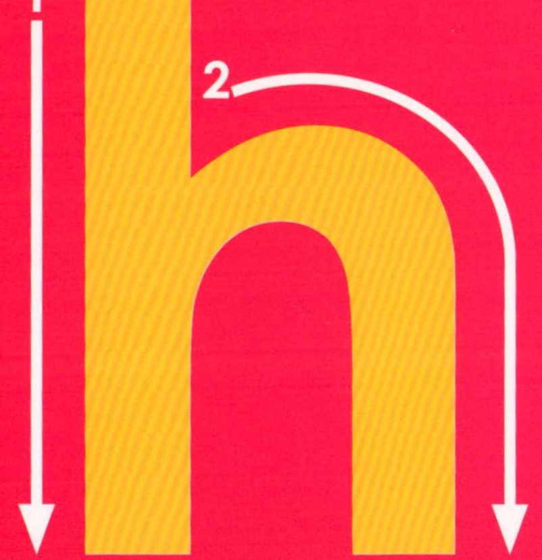

This is how you write it

The letter **h** can start many words.

horse

hawk

hippo

hot dog

hare

The letter h
can be inside
a word.
whale
three

shoes

chimp

shark

The letter h can be at the end of a word.

fish

laugh

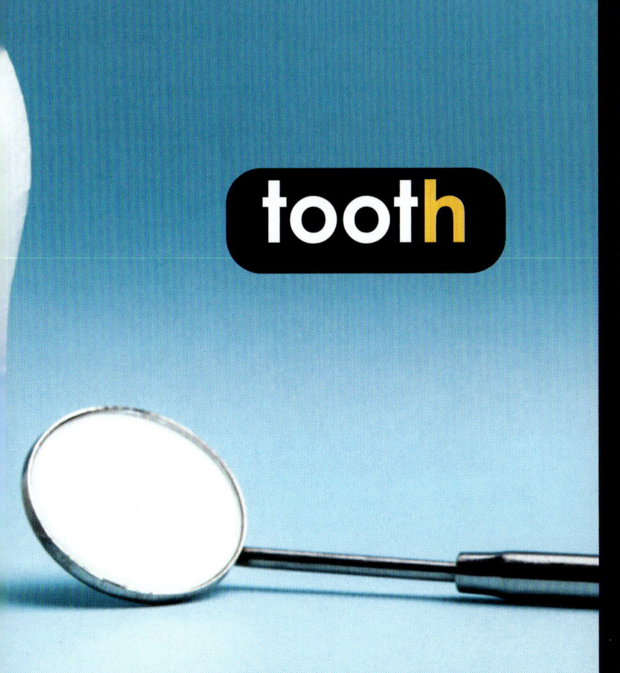
tooth

watch

Many names start with an uppercase H.

Harold plays in the rain.

Henry loves to write.

Helen likes balloons.

Heather is excited.

Hugh is a cowboy.

The letter **h** can make a sound or stay quiet.

Christmas

hand

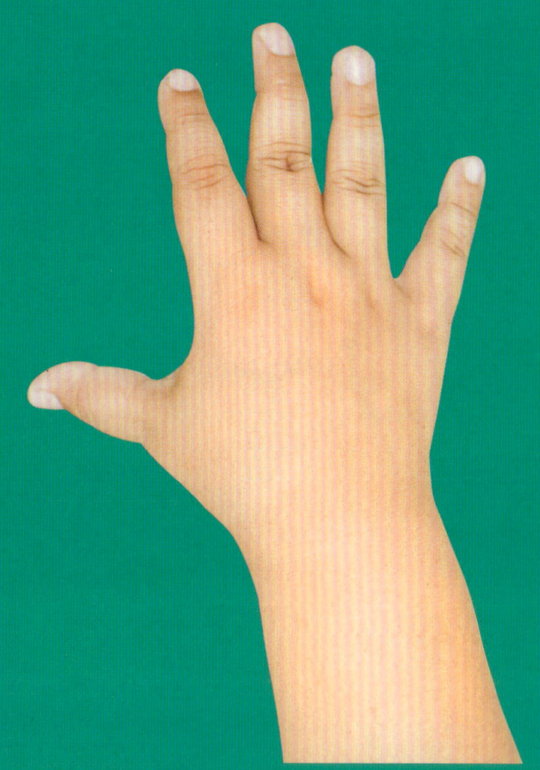

The letter h makes a sound in the word hand.

The letter h does not make a sound in the word Christmas.

The letter h makes a
sound in most words.
house

her
head
him
help

Sometimes the letter **h** does not make a sound.

cheetah

school

ghost

through

Having Fun with H

Hilda is having a horse party at her house.

She cooks hot dogs for her three friends from school.

Hank, Harry, and Hannah hold out their hooves. Hilda heaps hot dogs into their hooves.

They watch movies and laugh all night. Hilda laughs so hard she loses her tooth.

The alphabet has 26 letters.

H is the eighth letter in the alphabet.

Aa Bb Cc Dd

Ee Ff Gg **Hh** Ii Jj

Kk Ll Mm Nn Oo

Pp Qq Rr Ss Tt Uu

Vv Ww Xx Yy Zz

KEY WORDS

Research has shown that as much as 65 percent of all written material published in English is made up of 300 words. These 300 words cannot be taught using pictures or learned by sounding them out. They must be recognized by sight. This book contains 57 common sight words to help young readers improve their reading fluency and comprehension. This book also teaches young readers several important content words, such as proper nouns. These words are paired with pictures to aid in learning and improve understanding.

Page	Sight Words First Appearance
4	let, letter, the
5	a, an, how, is, it, this, write, you
6	can, many, start, words
8	be, three
10	at, Earth, end, of
11	watch
12	in, names, plays, with
13	likes, to
14	hand, make, or, sounds
15	does, not
16	house, most
17	head, help, her, him
18	sometimes
19	light, school, through
20	and, for, from, into, out, she, their
21	all, hard, night, so, they
22	has

Page	Content Words First Appearance
4	Hh
6	hawk, horse
7	hare, hippo, hot dog
8	whale
9	chimp, shark, shoes
11	fish, tooth
12	Harold, rain
13	balloons, cowboy, Heather, Helen, Henry, Hugh
14	Christmas
18	cheetah
19	ghost
20	friends, fun, Hank, Hannah, Harry, Hilda, hooves, party
21	movies
22	alphabet

Published by Smartbook Media Inc.
276 5th Avenue, Suite 704 #917
New York, NY 10001
Website: www.openlightbox.com

Library of Congress Cataloging-in-Publication Data

Names: Rylands, Warren, author. | Nugent, Samantha, author.
Title: Hh / Warren Rylands and Samantha Nugent.
Description: New York, NY : Smartbook Media Inc., [2022] | Series: Learn the ABCs | Audience: Grades K-1.
Identifiers: LCCN 2020054138 (print) | LCCN 2020054139 (ebook) | ISBN 9781510557567 (library binding) | ISBN 9781510557581 (ebook other)
Subjects: LCSH: English language--Consonants--Juvenile literature. | English literature--Alphabet--Juvenile literature.
Classification: LCC PE1165 .R9528 2022 (print) | LCC PE1165 (ebook) | DDC 428/.13--dc23
LC record available at https://lccn.loc.gov/2020054138
LC ebook record available at https://lccn.loc.gov/2020054139

Printed in Guangzhou, China
1 2 3 4 5 6 7 8 9 0 25 24 23 22 21

022021
110820

Art Director: Terry Paulhus **Project Coordinator:** Sara Cucini

The publisher acknowledges Getty Images as the primary image supplier for this title.